OUR GREAT STATES

WHAT'S GREAT ABOUT
NEBRASKA?

✸ Darice Bailer

LERNER PUBLICATIONS ✸ MINNEAPOLIS

CONTENTS

Content Consultant: Aaron Wilson, PhD.
Wilson researches independently and assists
nonprofit organizations with community-based
education initiatives.

Lerner Publications Company
A division of Lerner Publishing Group, Inc.
241 First Avenue North
Minneapolis, MN 55401 USA

For reading levels and more information, look
up this title at www.lernerbooks.com.

Main body text set in ITC Franklin Gothic Std
Book Condensed 12/15.
Typeface provided by Adobe Systems.

Library of Congress Cataloging-in-Publication
Data

Bailer, Darice.
    What's great about Nebraska? / by
Darice Bailer.
        pages cm. — (Our great states)
    Includes index.
    ISBN 978-1-4677-3870-5 (lib. bdg.
: alk. paper) — ISBN 978-1-4677-6094-2
(PB) — ISBN 978-1-4677-6272-4 (EB pdf)
    1. Nebraska—Juvenile literature. I. Title.
F666.3.B28 2015
978.2—dc23   2014024224

Manufactured in the United States of America
1 – PC – 12/31/14

NEBRASKA Welcomes You!

Nebraska is famous for its pioneer history and fossils. Hear tales of cowboys at the Great Platte River Road Archway. Climb aboard a covered wagon at Kreycik Riverview Elk & Buffalo Ranch. You can pretend you're moving west with your family. Look for monkeys, bats, and alligators at Omaha's Henry Doorly Zoo & Aquarium. Then cheer on the Huskers at Memorial Stadium at the University of Nebraska. There is something for everyone! Read more about the top ten things that make Nebraska great.

NEBRASKA ... the good life

Home of Arbor Day

WYOMING

PINE RIDGE

Niobrara River

SAND HILLS

SOUTH DAKOTA

Niobrara

Missouri River

IOWA

Panorama Point
(5,426 feet /
1,654 m)

Platte River

Norfolk

Columbus

Fremont

Omaha

Bellevue

North Platte

Grand
Island

Lincoln

Nebraska
City

Miles
0   20   40   60
0   40   80
Kilometers

N

Kearney

Hastings

COLORADO

KANSAS

Explore Nebraska's parks
and all the places in between!
Just turn the page to
find out about the
CORNHUSKER STATE. >

OMAHA'S HENRY DOORLY ZOO & AQUARIUM

Race across the footbridge in the jungle building and listen for the waterfall.

> Start your tour of Nebraska at Omaha's Henry Doorly Zoo & Aquarium. Make sure to wear your sneakers! You'll be doing a lot of walking. This is one of the largest zoos in the world. Explore Lied Jungle first. You'll see more than ninety different animals. Look for monkeys swinging from trees and hippos swimming in the water.

Next, make your way to Desert Dome. Snakes and lizards are a few of the animals to see. The lower level of the exhibit is home to many nocturnal animals. Walk through the caves. The bats squeak and fly above you. Then look for the hungry alligators in the swamp.

When your feet get tired, catch a ride on the Omaha Zoo Railroad. This ride will take you past many of the animals outside. Or maybe you'd like to ride the Skyfari. This chairlift takes you high above the animals. Look down and wave good-bye to the monkeys.

The Desert Dome at Henry Doorly Zoo holds the largest indoor desert exhibit.

STRATEGIC
AIR & SPACE MUSEUM

> Make your next Nebraska stop in Ashland at the Strategic Air & Space Museum. You can see airplanes, helicopters, and space shuttle simulators here. Don't be scared when you see a huge black spy plane at the museum's entrance. It looks as if it's diving right at you! The SR-71 was a very fast spy plane.

Sign up for a two-hour tour of the museum. Walk under the aircraft for up-close views. Climb into the cockpit of the B-52 bomber. Then learn more about Nebraska astronaut Clayton Anderson in the Heartland Astronaut exhibit.

Buy a ticket for the motion simulator ride. You can pretend to fly a helicopter. Or maybe you'd like to ride a roller coaster in space. If you're looking for more fun, check out the Space Shuttle Slide and Bouncer. Zip down the inflatable slide. Then tumble around in the bouncer. On your way out of the museum, buy some astronaut ice cream. It's so delicious that it'll send you to the moon!

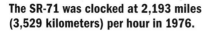
The SR-71 was clocked at 2,193 miles (3,529 kilometers) per hour in 1976.

Clayton Anderson is an engineer and a retired NASA astronaut. He is from Nebraska.

LINCOLN

> Lincoln is the capital of Nebraska. It's your next stop. The city is named after President Abraham Lincoln. If you visit the Nebraska State Capitol, look for a statue of Lincoln outside. The paintings inside the capitol illustrate Nebraska's history. Look for the black-and-white mural in the Great Hall. Then ride the elevator to the fourteenth floor. You'll have great views of the city from the observation deck.

Make your way to the Lincoln Children's Museum. Here you can pretend you're a TV reporter in the 10/11 TV Studio. Then learn how to take care of your pets in the Happy Healthy Pets exhibit. Pretend to be a prairie dog. You can crawl around a replica of an underground prairie dog tunnel.

After exploring the museum, head outside in the warmer months to enjoy the weather. Try golfing at Jim Ager Memorial Junior Golf Course. Professionals will teach you how to swing a club. Or they can help you become a better golfer if you've played before.

Daniel Freeman

THE HOMESTEAD ACT

President Lincoln signed the Homestead Act of 1862. This encouraged people to settle on western land. If families farmed the land for five years, they would receive 160 free acres (65 hectares) of land. Daniel Freeman was the first person to claim the free land in 1863. He settled in Beatrice.

Work on your golf skills at Jim Ager Memorial golf course while you're visiting Nebraska.

CHEER ON THE CORNHUSKERS!

> Imagine cheering for the Nebraska Cornhuskers inside their stadium in Lincoln. All around you are excited fans wearing red. The crowd is screaming. Soon you'll be standing up, raising your arms, and doing the wave. Nebraska has some of the most dedicated fans in college football. You can be one of them!

Join the University of Nebraska JV Team. This is the official kids' club of the Huskers. You'll receive a free red T-shirt for joining. You'll also get a free ticket to enjoy a spring football game. You can ask for a player's autograph during fall football camp. Shoot baskets during halftime at a basketball game. You can step up to bat at a baseball workshop too!

A few blocks from the football stadium is the University of Nebraska State Museum. You won't believe the saw like teeth on the giant shark. Be sure to check out the ancient swords and spears too.

CORN PRODUCTION

Nebraska's soil is ideal for growing corn and soybeans. Corn is the state's most important crop. Nebraska is the third-largest corn-producing state in the United States. No wonder Nebraska's nickname is the Cornhusker State. A cornhusker is a person who peels the green husks off an ear of corn.

Be sure to wear your foam corn hat, along with your red T-shirt, to a Cornhuskers game!

ASHFALL FOSSIL BEDS STATE HISTORICAL PARK

> Millions of years ago, animals lived around a waterhole near the city of Royal. But almost 12 million years ago, a volcano erupted in present-day Idaho. Heavy winds spread the ashes all the way to what is now Nebraska. Prehistoric rhinoceroses, horses, and camels ate the ash-covered grass and died.

You can see fossils of these animals at Ashfall Fossil Beds State Historical Park. Their skeletons are buried in rock. Stop in the Hubbard Rhino Barn. Whole skeletons were discovered and left in the ground for visitors to see. What animals do you see? You may spot a camel or a mother rhino and her calf.

Examine the many different fossils in the barn. The paleontologists who work there invite you to ask questions. They're there to teach. Pick up a brush and pretend to be a paleontologist at your own pretend dig. See what skeletons you uncover.

At Hubbard Rhino Barn, you'll see many fossils from ancient animals, including rhinos.

RHINO CALF "T. L."
EST. AGE, 1 YEAR
ALL MILK TEETH IN WEAR

15

KREYCIK RIVERVIEW ELK & BUFFALO RANCH

> Next on your journey through Nebraska is the Kreycik Riverview Elk & Buffalo Ranch. It is in Niobrara. This ranch is home to herds of elk and buffalo. Take a covered wagon tour. The staff gives you ears of corn to feed the elk, the buffalo, and their calves. Feel the buffalo nibble the corn out of your palm. Then pet the elk calf. You may hear it make lots of noises. During the summer, watch out for outlaws. Your wagon can get held up in an Old West show!

Drive to Niobrara State Park after your wagon tour. It is 8 miles (13 km) away. Here you can float down the Niobrara River on a tube. The river winds through canyons and beautiful waterfalls. Be on the lookout for wildlife. Maybe you will spot a bald eagle. You may even see an osprey diving in the river. Watch to see if it catches a fish with its claws!

CATTLE RANCHES

Nebraska has huge cattle ranches. Farms and ranches cover about 90 percent of the state. Nebraska supplies more beef to grocery stores than any other state in the nation. It is also famous for its steak restaurants.

You will see buffalo up close at
Kreycik Riverview Elk & Buffalo Ranch.

NEBRASKA CITY

> Pack a picnic basket and head for Arbor Day Farm in Nebraska City. When you arrive, scramble up the steps to the top of the Canopy Tree House. You'll be 50 feet (15 meters) high. Down below, you can hike a trail and run across two wooden bridges. Hop on the Discovery Ride for a one-hour train ride through the orchards. When you leave the farm, you'll receive a present. It's a tree seedling for you to plant at home.

After your picnic, visit the Lewis & Clark Missouri River Visitors Center. Learn about the two famous explorers: Meriwether Lewis and William Clark. They traveled through Nebraska on their way to the Pacific Ocean in 1804. A movie tells you more about them. It also shows you what Nebraska wilderness was like more than two hundred years ago. Lewis and Clark wrote in their journals about 122 animals. See displays of these animals in the Hall of Animals. A life-size black bear and cub are just two of the animals you may see. Push a button and hear the grizzly bear growl!

Climb aboard a replica of one of Lewis and Clark's boats outside. You may see workers dressed up like the explorers. They tell how the explorers built their winter fort.

ARBOR DAY

A Nebraskan named Julius Sterling Morton loved trees. He knew how important they were for shade, wood, and holding soil in place. That was especially important in Nebraska because it was treeless and flat. So in 1872, Morton set up a special tree-planting day. It is now a national holiday called Arbor Day.

Arbor Day Farm has plenty of space to spread out a quilt and enjoy a picnic lunch.

CENTRAL NEBRASKA

> Have you ever wondered what life was like for pioneers? See for yourself at the Great Platte River Road Archway near Kearney. Watch a short movie about the 1800s. You'll learn more about old wagon routes heading west. It will seem like the Pony Express riders and the buffalo are jumping out of the screen!

After the movie, walk through the museum. Strap on headphones and listen as a recording by actors tells you about the life of a settler. If you're looking for more fun, head outside to the TrailBlaze Maze. Follow the clues as you race through the twists and turns.

Approximately 20 miles (32 km) away is Rowe Sanctuary. Each spring, you can see more than half a million cranes stop here. Sign up to watch the cranes with a guide after sunset. Be sure to dress warm! It can be chilly when the sun isn't shining.

THE PONY EXPRESS

The Pony Express delivered mail for eighteen months from 1860 to 1861. Brave young men rode ponies 1,966 miles (3,164 km) from Saint Joseph, Missouri, to Sacramento, California. The trip took approximately ten days one way. There were Pony Express stations in Nebraska. Riders could rest and eat here. In October 1861, the Pony Express was no longer needed. The telegraph system, which transmitted messages over wires, replaced it.

The Archway museum looks like an old covered bridge over the highway. Cars and trucks can still drive under it.

FORT ROBINSON STATE PARK

> Fort Robinson State Park in Harrison is Nebraska's largest state park. Start the morning with a wagon ride. Then enjoy an outdoor breakfast of pancakes, ham, and eggs. Later, saddle up a horse and ride the trails.

You'll want to drop by the Trailside Museum of Natural History in the park. More than ten thousand years ago, two mammoths locked their tusks in battle. Then they fell to the ground and died. Hunt for their skeletons in the museum. Then look for the huge skull of a mosasaur. This was a giant sea lizard that swam in the sea that once covered Nebraska.

Still hunting for fossils? Look for the strange beast that had the skull of a large horse, long front legs, short back legs, and three curved claws on each foot. It was called a moropus. You can find it at the Agate Fossil Beds National Monument.

Have you ever wanted to land on the moon? You'll feel as if you're there at Toadstool Geologic Park. Hike a 1-mile (1.6 km) trail. See how wind and water erosion carved away the sandstone. It made cool rock formations.

Along with fossils, you'll also see wildlife at Agate Fossil Beds National Monument, including white-tailed deer fawns.

You can hitch a ride on the red stagecoach at Fort Robinson State Park.

CHIMNEY ROCK NATIONAL HISTORIC SITE

> If you were a pioneer kid, you heard stories about Chimney Rock. This rock looks like a chimney. Erosion caused its shape. It was the most famous landmark heading west. Your horse-drawn wagon might reach it after weeks of hard travel. Make this your final stop on your trip through Nebraska.

Stop at the Chimney Rock National Historic Site in Bayard. A short video tells what it was like traveling west. Next, have fun in the Load the Wagon exhibit. Decide what to take on your journey west. You'll find food, furniture, and other pioneer belongings to choose from. Load up the wagon. A red light flashes when it's full!

Make your way to Scotts Bluff National Monument. Ride to the peak in a car or a shuttle bus. Or hike on your own two feet! You could pass a park ranger dressed like a fur trader. An actor playing a Pony Express rider might gallop past you with the mail.

At the top of Scotts Bluff, you can see for miles across the flat prairie. Nebraska is a sea of grass and wide-open spaces. Wave good-bye to Nebraska from here!

At Scotts Bluff National Monument, you'll see many rock formations, including Eagle Rock.

You will see actors dressed as pioneers at Chimney Rock National Historic Site.

YOUR TOP TEN!

You've just read about ten fun things to do and see in Nebraska. Now it's your turn! Imagine you're planning a trip to Nebraska. What would your top ten list include? What places in Nebraska would you most like to see? Grab a sheet of paper, and jot down your Nebraska top ten list. You can make it into a book. Just add drawings or pictures from the Internet.

> MAP KEY

- ⬟ Capital city
- ◯ City
- ◎ Point of interest
- ▲ Highest elevation
- –·– State border

WYOMING

PINE RIDGE

Niobrara River

SAND HILLS

Scotts Bluff National Monument (Gering)

Chimney Rock National Historic Site (Bayard)

Platte River

Panorama Point (5,426 feet/ 1,654 m)

Miles
0   20   40   60
0   40   80
Kilometers

COLORADO

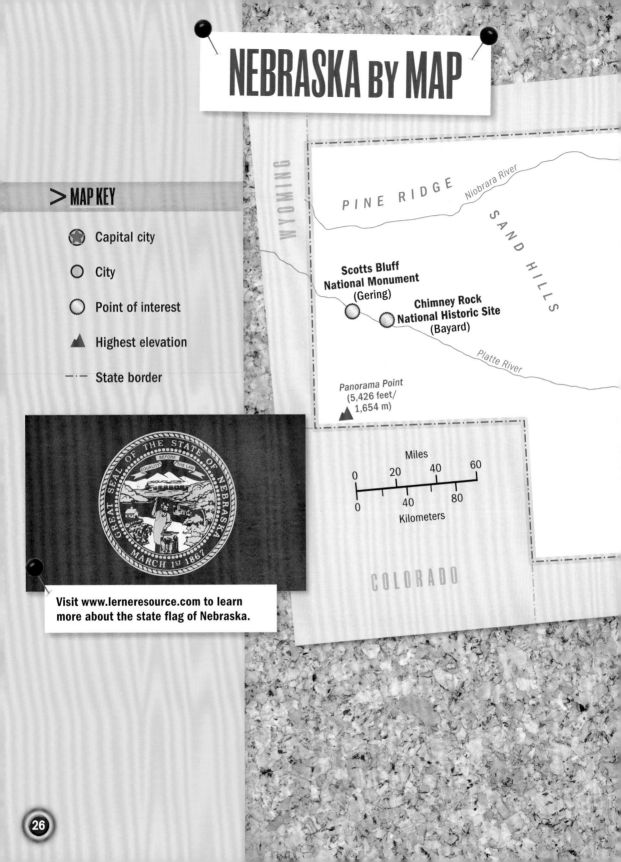

Visit www.lernerresource.com to learn more about the state flag of Nebraska.

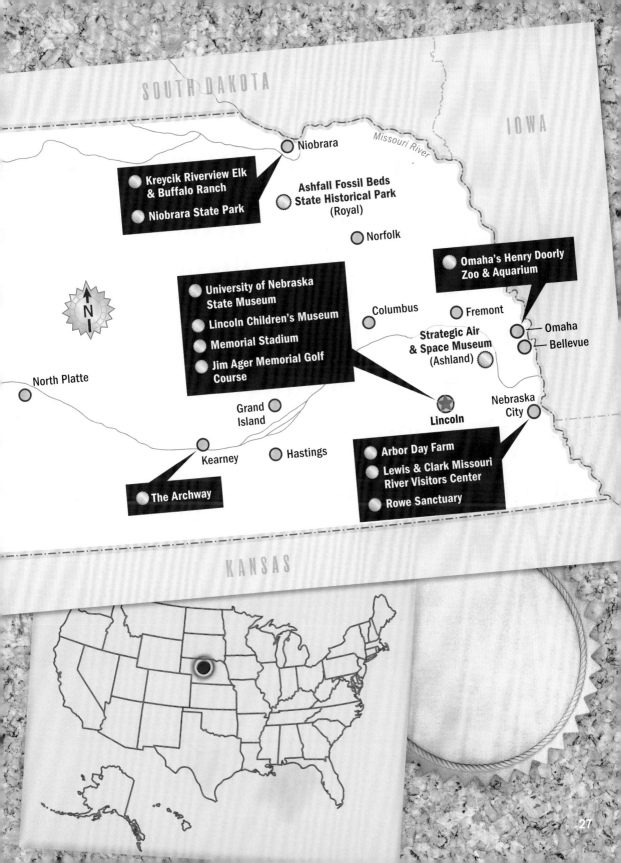

SOUTH DAKOTA

IOWA

Missouri River

Niobrara

Kreycik Riverview Elk & Buffalo Ranch

Niobrara State Park

Ashfall Fossil Beds State Historical Park (Royal)

Norfolk

Omaha's Henry Doorly Zoo & Aquarium

University of Nebraska State Museum

Lincoln Children's Museum

Memorial Stadium

Jim Ager Memorial Golf Course

N

Columbus

Fremont

Strategic Air & Space Museum (Ashland)

Omaha

Bellevue

North Platte

Grand Island

Lincoln

Nebraska City

Kearney

Hastings

Arbor Day Farm

Lewis & Clark Missouri River Visitors Center

Rowe Sanctuary

The Archway

KANSAS

NEBRASKA FACTS

NICKNAME: The Cornhusker State

SONG: "Beautiful Nebraska" by Jim Fras and Guy G. Miller

MOTTO: "Equality Before the Law"

> FLOWER: giant goldenrod

TREE: eastern cottonwood

> BIRD: western meadowlark

ANIMAL: white-tailed deer

FOOD: beef

DATE AND RANK OF STATEHOOD: March 1, 1867; the 37th state

> CAPITAL: Lincoln

AREA: 77,349 square miles (200,333 sq. km)

AVERAGE JANUARY TEMPERATURE: 23°F (–5°C)

AVERAGE JULY TEMPERATURE: 76°F (24°C)

POPULATION AND RANK: 1,868,516; 37th (2013)

MAJOR CITIES AND POPULATIONS: Omaha (421,570), Lincoln (265,404), Bellevue (52,604), Grand Island (49,989), Kearney (31,790)

NUMBER OF US CONGRESS MEMBERS: 3 representatives, 2 senators

NUMBER OF ELECTORAL VOTES: 5

NATURAL RESOURCES: petroleum, sand, gravel, clay, limestone

> AGRICULTURAL PRODUCTS: beef cattle, corn, hogs, milk, soybeans, wheat

MANUFACTURED GOODS: chemicals, food products, machinery, medical equipment

STATE HOLIDAYS AND CELEBRATIONS: Pioneers' Memorial Day, Nebraska Czech Day, American Indian Day

GLOSSARY

cockpit: the area in a plane where the pilot sits

exhibit: a collection of objects that have been put out in a public space for people to look at

mammoth: a large, hairy elephant that lived in ancient times

nocturnal: active mainly during the night

observation: designed for use in viewing something

paleontologist: a person who studies fossils and ancient life

prairie: a large area of flat or rolling grassland

sanctuary: a place where something is protected or given shelter

simulator: a machine that is used to show what something looks or feels like

telegraph: an electric device for sending messages across long distances

LERNER

SOURCE

Expand learning beyond the printed book. Download free, complementary educational resources for this book from our website, www.lerneresource.com.

FURTHER INFORMATION

Ashfall Fossil Beds State Historical Park
http://ashfall.unl.edu/educators.html
Read the ten coolest facts about Nebraska's ancient fossil beds. This website features crossword puzzles and coloring sheets about ancient animals you've never heard of.

Figley, Mary Rhodes. *The Prairie Adventure of Sarah and Annie, Blizzard Survivors.* Minneapolis: Graphic Universe, 2012. The worst blizzard sisters Sarah and Annie can remember tears the roof off their schoolhouse in Nebraska in 1888. Can their teacher lead them through the blinding snowstorm and darkness to safety?

Nebraska State Capitol
http://capitol.org/files/scavenger-hunt.pdf
When you visit the Nebraska State Capitol in Lincoln, print out this scavenger hunt to find out all the tributes to our sixteenth president.

Shepherd, Rajean Luebs. *Husker Numbers: A Nebraska Number Book.* Chelsea, MI: Sleeping Bear Press, 2007. Learn countless facts about Nebraska's pioneer history and its many treasures, from ancient fossil sights to the Henry Doorly Zoo & Aquarium.

University of Nebraska State Museum
http://museum.unl.edu/exhibits/index.html
Click on the exhibits and travel back in time. See pictures of hunting spears hundreds of years old.

Yolen, Jane. *Elsie's Bird.* New York: Philomel Books, 2010. Elsie is sad when her mama dies. Then she moves with her father to the Nebraska frontier. She begins to see how beautiful the prairie is when she meets a canary named Timmy Tune.

INDEX

PHOTO ACKNOWLEDGMENTS

The images in this book are used with the permission of: © dustin77a/Shutterstock Images, p. 1; NASA, pp. 2–3, 9 (bottom); © Spirit of America/Shutterstock Images, pp. 4, 17, 24–25; © Laura Westlund/Independent Picture Service, pp. 5 (top), 26–27; © Sharon Day/Shutterstock Images, p. 5 (bottom); © Bill Grant/Alamy, p. 6; © iStock/Thinkstock, pp. 6–7, 7; © Walter Bibikow Danita Delimont Photography/Newscom, pp. 8–9, 9 (top); © Katherine Welles/Shutterstock Images, pp. 10–11; © Thinkstock, p. 11; Library of Congress, pp. 10 (LC-USZ62-104167), 19 (LC-USZ62-14802) (top), 20 (LC-DIG-highsm-23442), 29 (LC-DIG-highsm-04814) (bottom right); © Weldon Schloneger/Shutterstock Images, p. 12; © Zumapress/Icon SMI, pp. 12–13; © Zach Bolinger/Icon SMI, p. 13; Carl Malamud, pp. 14–15; © Dave G. Houser/Corbis, p. 15; © Jorg Hackemann/Shutterstock Images, p. 16; © Chuck Haney/Danita Delimont Photography/Newscom, pp. 16–17, 22–23; © Dave Weaver/AP Images, pp. 18–19; © Lynn Seldon/Danita Delimont Photography/Newscom, p. 19 (bottom); © Nebraska Game and Parks/KRT/Newscom, pp. 20–21; © Henryk Sadura/Shutterstock Images, p. 21; © Visions of America, LLC/Alamy, p. 23 (bottom); National Park Service, pp. 23 (top), 25 (top); © Greg Ryan/Alamy, p. 25 (bottom); © nicoolay/iStockphoto, p. 26; © GlOck/Shutterstock Images, p. 29 (top right); © Matt Knoth/Shutterstock Images, p. 29 (top left); © Zeljko Radojko/Shutterstock Images, p. 29 (bottom left).

Cover images: © Mark Newman/Lonely Planet Images/Getty Images (Elephant Hall); © Eric Francis/Stringer/Getty Images (Nebraska Cornhuskers); © Diana Robinson Photography/Moment Open/Getty Images (sandhill cranes); © Laura Westlund/Independent Picture Service (map); © iStockphoto.com/fpm (seal); © iStockphoto.com/vicm (pushpins); © iStockphoto.com/benz190 (corkboard).